JOURNEY TOWARDS HOLISTIC LEADERSHIP

PART - 1

AF529431

JOURNEY TOWARDS HOLISTIC LEADERSHIP

PART - 1

Vivek Mehta

Worldwide Published by

Pendown Press

PENDOWN PRESS LLP

An ISO 9001 & ISO 14001 Certified Co.,

Regd. Office: 3767A, Kanhaiya Nagar,
Tri Nagar, Delhi-110035

Ph.: 8130886000, 9650072927

E-mail: info@pendownpress.com

Branch Office: 1A/2A, 20, Hari Sadan, Ansari Road,
Daryaganj, New Delhi-110002

Ph.: 011-45794768

Website: PendownPress.com

Edition: 2025

Price: ₹ 251

ISBN: 978-93-5554-803-0

Layout and Cover Designed by Pendown Graphics Team

Printed and Bound in India by Thomson Press India Ltd.

Dedication

This book is dedicated to my wife, Smt. Madhvi Mehta, my son, Krish Mehta, my daughter, Kashish Mehta.

Table of Contents

FOUR PROMISES FROM THE READER

I'm creating this workbook so that you can feel and experience everything I've felt, every milestone I've reached, and every lesson I've learned. That's my intention. But before you dive in, I want to ask for four promises from you—promises that will guide you as you explore and grow.

First, be open and empty. Imagine a container left upside down in the rain—it can't collect a single drop of water. Likewise, if your mind is already filled with preconceived ideas, it will be hard for anything new to enter. To truly absorb this knowledge, you need to let go of what you think you already know. Approach this with a clear mind, open to fresh insights and ideas. Let go of the old to make space for the new. If you can do that, you'll be able to see life from a fresh perspective and, hopefully, use these insights in meaningful ways.

Second, listen carefully. Often, our minds are scattered, constantly buzzing with thoughts, drifting here and there. In this journey. I'm asking you to really focus, to listen with intent, and to engage fully in every task. It's a promise to stay present, to let each word and lesson sink in without distraction.

Third, act consciously. Whatever you do, be fully there. Don't let your thoughts wander elsewhere. Give each task the attention it deserves, with your awareness completely in the moment.

Finally, share what you've learned. If this knowledge brings even the slightest shift in your life, share it. Pass it on to others who may need it, especially those in your community who strive to make a difference without asking for anything in return. That's the last promise I'm asking of you: take what you learn here and pay it forward, so others may also benefit and grow.

With these promises, I believe you're ready to start this journey with me.

Take a moment now: Write down the promises you are making to yourself in this exercise book. Read them every morning as a reminder of your commitment to growth and transformation.

1.

2.

3.

Each morning, take a few moments to go over these promises and focus on them. Practice them diligently for a week, and whenever your mind starts to wander, gently remind yourself of these commitments.

FOUR QUESTIONS FROM LIFE

Friends, in our busy lives, we're constantly rushing, chasing comfort, wealth, and various goals, just getting through each day. But have we really taken the time to understand our lives deeply, to recognize its true essence from within? There are four essential questions that I believe are the foundational principles of knowing and understanding life. If you can fully grasp these questions, you'll find yourself closer to winning the inner battle of life. You'll experience more happiness, health, and joy.

These four questions are thoughtfully selected from my own experiences. To truly understand life, I encourage you to work through these questions with your whole heart. Reflect on them, write about them, and immerse yourself in them fully. Before we begin with the first question, I want to revisit the four promises we discussed. So, what are these promises? They are, in essence, deep commitments to yourself.

First Promise – Be Eligible.

What does it mean to be eligible? I'd like to share a story to illustrate this. There was a devoted disciple of Mahatma Buddha named Anand. One day, he asked, "Guruji, you teach so many people about meditation and guide them toward enlightenment. Why then don't all of them achieve it? Why don't they find peace and happiness?"

Mahatma Buddha's response was profound. He said, "A container turned upside down in the rain can never fill itself. Similarly, unless a disciple empties his mind, he cannot fully receive." So, the first promise is to let go of what you think you know about life, to clear your mind of past knowledge so that you're truly open to new insights.

Second Promise – Listen and Focus.

The mind is naturally restless. When we try to focus, there's always background chatter that pulls us away. So, the second promise is to bring your full attention to the moment, to listen and focus deeply without letting your mind wander. Only then can you begin to experience clarity and fulfillment in life.

Third Promise – Act Consciously.

In whatever you do, be fully present. Commit to engaging with awareness in each task so that your mind is fully in tune with your actions.

Fourth Promise – Share with Society.

Whatever you gain from this journey, share it freely with those who can benefit. Pass on your knowledge without expecting anything in return, giving back to society with an open heart.

If you keep these promises, you'll be ready to embark on this journey with a clearer, more open perspective.

FIRST QUESTION

What is Life?

The first question: What is life? Friends, this is a very profound question. It can have different opinions, different perspectives. I'm leaving this paragraph empty here so that you can explore your own viewpoint on life.

Question – What is life?

If I may share my thoughts, in my opinion, life is a journey between two important milestones. The first milestone is when we begin to breathe (the time of birth), and the second milestone is our final breath (the time of death).

Philosophy of life in one sentence, but to know it in detail we will have to go deeper.

Contrary to popular belief, life is not just about hustle and earning money. Nor is it about taking retirement and going to the top of a mountain. Life also doesn't mean simply spending time with family without any purpose or goal.

Friends, the construction of the wheel of life involves many components coming together. It requires proper coordination of all aspects. When there is an excess of one thing and neglect of another, its balance is disrupted, and everything falls apart. So today, I will tell you about the wheel of life. The wheel of life is like the wheels of a car. Just like there is an inner rim and an outer tire in the car's wheel, life also has a similar structure.

In its inner rim, there are the body, mind, and soul. It is their strength that brings strength to the tire (outer) and enables the wheel of life to move smoothly.

The outer covering (tire) is also made up of three things - your work, your family, and your society.

So you need to understand all these (6) components thoroughly and strengthen them. It is important for you to understand that if any one of these 6 elements becomes weak, the speed of this wheel-like life will decrease, and you may be deprived of living a wonderful and lively life.

FIRST ASPECT: BODY

So first of all friends----The first aspect is your body. Remember, your body is a reflection of your inner strength. It shows your physical and mental power. People can understand from your body whether you are diseased or healthy. Apart from physical health, your mental health is also important.

Mental health is related to your habits, your emotions, and your ability to think (positive thinking). It is the indicator of your likes and dislikes. It shows feelings of hatred, negative emotions, and other disorders. Additionally, it also indicates your ability to control your state of mind in adverse situations. If your mental health is good, you will stay away from negative emotions and thoughts and will also have a strong willpower. Even in difficult situations, you will not be shaken. With a calm mind, you can confidently navigate the turbulent waves of life's ocean, facing challenges fearlessly.

If you stay healthy in every way, you'll enjoy your work, savor the pleasures of your body, travel anywhere, and live life to the fullest.

So what will you have to do for this----- You will have to eat good food, exercise regularly, and maintain a positive mindset so that your mental state remains good.

Friends, health is that treasure which once lost, you cannot get it back. I have also felt this in my life. During the golden years of his life, I was only focused on work and neglected my health. So friends, once health is lost, it takes a lot of effort to get it back. Still it can't come back the way it was. You see today, no matter which hospital it is, it is full of patients. Every fourth person is suffering from mental illness. So, friends, just think for a moment, what do you do in the 24 hours of the day to keep your body healthy? (Exercise, yoga, meditation, running, eating well, playing, etc.).

1-

2-

3-

4-

5-

6-

7-

SECOND ASPECT: MIND

The second aspect of life is the mind. As there is a saying, "Conquer the Mind, Conquer the World." If you have conquered your mind, you have conquered the entire world. Mind is also of two types---conscious mind and subconscious mind. Many books have been written on this subject. Like: "The Power of Your Subconscious Mind," (Joseph Murphy) on the powers of the mind, on mind powers, what are the powers of the mind, what are the powers of the conscious mind, what are the powers of the subconscious mind, etc. etc.

Will not talk about this too briefly. All we can say is that if the mind desires, it can turn a common person into a billionaire, can make a wonderful human being. It can bring about so much change in a human being that there is no limit.

Mind not only gives us knowledge and wisdom, it also paves the way for our progress, transforms us from dust to rock and gives us such a great personality which almost everyone aspires to achieve.

Our mind is really amazing. We just have to understand the powers (mind) within us and awaken them. So there is a need to recognize the powers of the mind. Books, the internet, and YouTube videos can be useful mediums for this recognition.

But now we will talk about how you can shape your life through your mind. So you can accept your knowledge, your wisdom through your mind. Many people say that it is very cerebral when you absorb knowledge. What does this mean? That is, he is very diligent towards his work, his knowledge is very good, he has a lot of skill.

Friends, this is the greatest strength of the mind. To develop your mind, you need to embrace knowledge and acquire skills in life. In your life, your mind should be like a powerful tool, supporting you, helping you grasp knowledge. For this, every effort must be made. If you can achieve something significant by using your mind positively, nothing can be bigger than that.

So we will understand the function of the mind and use it to increase our knowledge and skills. We will work on the subjects in which you have to get knowledge and skills.

Friends, write briefly in which areas you want to increase your knowledge. In which areas do you want to increase your skills? So you write 5-6 points. There is no need to write too many points, friends.

1-

2-

3-

4-

5-

6-

This is an exercise book that you have to read again and again, work on it again and again. You can also write down 3 to 4 points about which areas you need to increase your knowledge and skills to improve your life.

Friends---- after writing this on this, you each make your own plan--- after this. Make a plan for every month. Make a plan for every day. Make a plan for every week. So, when you make a plan and spend at least 2 hours in the 24 hours of your life in improving the mind and increasing the powers of the mind, then friends, your life will be a good one, you will live a complete life.

Identify the powers of your mind, friends! And note whatever areas you want to gain knowledge from and make a complete plan to work on them. You can make a weekly plan, a monthly plan or an annual plan.

You can set your goals. So, the biggest function of the mind in your life is to enhance knowledge and wisdom. After that, there are many other powers that you can use for good deeds.

So, in the end, I would say that if you win your mind, you win the world. You have to conquer the world, and for that, you need to have big goals in life. You have to live a happy life. What you are going to present to people in the exercise book is not only the art of knowing your life but also the art of living it.

So friends, the second aspect is the mind. It should be your intention to concentrate the mind, recognize the powers of the mind and increase your knowledge and skills through the mind, and then take it to the highest level should be your aspiration.

Out of your 24 hours, give some time, at least two hours, to those activities which will improve your knowledge and skills.

If you work hard regularly, the results will be miraculously beneficial. As the saying goes-

"Karat Karat Abhyas Ke, Jadamati Hot Sujaan,
Rassi Aawat Jaat Te, Sil Par Padat Nishaan."

Meaning that with continuous efforts even a foolish man can become intelligent. Just as by repeatedly rubbing the rope on the stone of the well's pulley (parapet), the stone also gets marked.

"In reality, the rope cannot cut the stone,
but due to consistent rubbing there,
the edges of the well's pulley become
grooved, creating a hole in that spot."

So, friends, when you give your regular time to this mind to increase your knowledge and skills, then your life will become a joyful one because whoever is knowledgeable, whoever is skillful, his future is very good and he can achieve success in his profession.

THIRD ASPECT: SOUL

Now we are going to talk about the third aspect of the innermost part of life. The inner part of the wheel of life is made up of soul, body and mind. As we have talked about body and mind, now we are going to talk about soul.

What is soul? And what are its strengths? The irony in this context is that many people don't even work in the realm of the soul. They think there's nothing there. However, perhaps these people are unaware of the infinite powers of the soul, do not know its universality. If you recognize the powers of the soul and work on enhancing them, your inner strength will grow, and you will achieve purity. Soul and God! What is the role of the soul? The soul is nothing but a small part of God.

The Supreme Power that runs the universe, the force behind everything, is what we call God. And the small part of it that resides within our bodies is the soul, as said by Lord Krishna in the Bhagavad Gita...

नैनं छिन्दन्ति शस्त्राणि नैनं दहति पावकः।
न चैनं क्लेदयन्त्यापो न शोषयति मारुतः

Meaning of this Shloka: In the Bhagwad Gita, Lord Krishna expounds the nature of the atma and tells Arjuna – The atma cannot be shattered by weapons, it cannot be burnt by fires, it cannot be drenched by the waters and it cannot be rendered dry by the winds.

The soul never dies; it simply moves from one body to another.

So, my friends, many books have been written on the soul, but more than books, it can be understood through experiences. It's essential to feel it. It is very important to understand it by introspection. To increase the powers of the soul, first, you must understand its qualities, what the soul really is?

The most significant fact about the soul is that it is our friend. It is powerful, fearless, and free from deceit. It is untouched by all forms of illusion.

There is a need to understand it. Consciousness towards oneself. You can increase the qualities of this soul by meditation, pranayam and taking care of yourself. You can make it your best friend and greatest guide. As your soul becomes purer, you'll gradually connect with God. And as your purity increases, you'll become closer to God. Friends, the day your soul becomes so pure, you'll have no fear of anything, and worries won't bother you. You'll feel that you are powerful, free from deceit, untouched by illusion, and unaffected by greed. And when you feel this, you'll connect with God and on the same day that event will happen which is called enlightenment, my friends.

So, you also need to work on this soul, which is the third aspect of knowing life. However, it's unfortunate to see that many people neglect it; nobody works on it. If you truly understand the qualities of the soul and invest your time and energy in nurturing those qualities, then I can confidently say that you can become one of the best person in this world.

And to understand this power, I am giving you a small example...The one who wrote the Quran, his name was Prophet Muhammad. He was not educated. He used to go to the cave of Hira for the peace of his soul. When this incident happened to him, which is called enlightenment or revelation, on that day the Quran was revealed to him. So, friends, when this incident happens, an amazing transformation comes into your life. Many organizations are working to achieve this transformation, many gurus are involved, but many people get lost in the middle.

So friends, increase the power of your soul... and meditate. Meditation is the art through which you can connect your soul with God... many types of meditation, many methods have been taught by Osho, Sri Sri Ravi Shankar, Sadhguru, and others.

They have suggested some methods... you should check all the methods... some method will surely be suitable for you.

So, the most important thing is to engage in satsang, to work on your soul after listening to satsang, to work on the qualities of the soul, to understand the qualities of the soul, and to bridge the gap between the soul and yourself, transforming yourself into that pure soul.

Friends, this is a practice book for you. In this, first of all you will write what are the qualities of the soul, which you read above, you write them and secondly, after introspecting, write what qualities the soul that is inside you today possesses and you What work needs to be done to develop which qualities?

So, friends, make a plan and write it down. If you know meditation techniques, then meditate. If not, then try to develop an interest in various techniques. To connect with a Sadguru and for the purification of the soul, Guru is the bridge which can connect the soul to God.

But do not stop on the bridge. Keep walking on it continuously. I have seen many things too. I have visited many organizations. I listen to the thoughts of the Brahma Kumaris. I have also meditated with Sri Sri. So, don't stop anywhere. Whenever you find a path, keep moving forward. Remember—meditation is the method that will connect your soul with God. The effort and hard work you need to put in for the purification of the soul, you will do it through satsang.

So, friends, I have told you about the soul and how to increase your self-power. With this, the third segment ends here.

FOURTH ASPECT: WORK

The fourth part of life, or the fourth aspect of life. Friends, in the first three parts, we have explored the inner aspects - the body, mind, and soul. After understanding them, now we move towards the external aspects of life. This external aspect plays a crucial role in our lives. So, let's introduce you with this fourth pillar. The fourth part of life is work, or employment.

Now, it's important to understand here that work doesn't just mean sleeping, waking up, etc. Work refers to what is necessary for your livelihood.

How crucial is work in life, friends—today, we are living with our families, managing households, and living within families. For their upkeep and to fulfill our dreams, it is very, very important for us to work. Without work, the wheels of the chariot of life come to a halt, our self-esteem is lost, and its relevance diminishes.

So, what is the most important aspect of work? The part of our lives that we spend after waking up— that is work. Our work provides us with wealth. Work is the source of wealth. Work gives us respect, honor, and more. It could be government employment, working for a private company or firm, or even self-employment.

So, it is very important to self-reflect on what we should do for the betterment of the place in which we spend most of our life, how to achieve excellence in it. Friends, it is very important to bring perfection within us to work, it is very important to be efficient in work.

Work is something everyone does. Some are successful, some are very successful, while others may struggle or fall into the category of beginners. So, what do we need to do to be successful? For that, we need introspection. In my opinion, the most crucial aspect of bringing proficiency to work is how much time you devote to it.

It depends on your situation and what you want to do. Typically, we should give 7 to 9 hours to work. And to work, we need various skills and abilities –

1. First of all, it is important for us to have leadership quality for our work.
2. It is important for us to be passionate about our work.
3. Thirdly, it is important to have time management.

Having leadership qualities is indeed crucial, but it's equally important to have passion and effective time management skills.

If you pay attention to these three aspects, you will be able to use your 24 hours properly and make good use of them. You will be able to bring better output from your work and will also be able to establish a balance between work and your personal life.

First and foremost, you need to develop leadership qualities. Know this leadership. Assume that you are a leader. You lead an organization, you lead your team, you lead your family. So it is very important to have leadership qualities. It is very important to know what leadership is, to know its attitude and perception, what values it has, what qualities it has, it is very important to know them all.

The second is passion. If we look at passion, it's often called "junoon" in Hindi. So, if you're doing something, and you don't have that junoon or passion for it, then you won't be serious about your work. As a result, you won't be able to excel in it, and gradually, it will become a burden for you. Soon, you'll want to get rid of it, or you might even be fired. You'll never be able to fit into the category of successful people. So achieving mastery in work is the basic mantra of success. If you do any work without passion, you will neither enjoy it nor will you be able to reach the point in life that you want to achieve through work.

So, friends, you also need to do a lot of studying for passion. You'll have to read books, watch videos. You have to understand passion. Let me give you a small but valuable formula. Whatever subject you want to generate passion for, choose only 2 questions about that subject per day and search for the answers to those two questions through any medium and write them down in your diary. And as your knowledge grows, your passion will also increase. So this one small formula will increase your passion towards that subject, towards that job, towards that work to which you give most time in life. With the money you get for giving that time, you run your family and want to run the society, take care of your body. Yes, friends, the supply of wealth will come from work itself.

FIFTH ASPECT: FAMILY

Friends, this fifth part is very important, and it's called family. Family is a group of people who support you in fulfilling your dreams, your desires, and in return, they only want one thing from you - quality time, good moments.

However, there are many people who ignore their families because of work (or carrying the burden of work). Perhaps they do this because they don't realize the importance of family, or they simply overlook it. But believe me, family is as important as work, in fact family is more important than work.

Let's understand this with an example. Suppose a person has a lot of work, a big business, and as a result, he is earning a lot of money. But if he fails to give time to his family (for the sake of money), then his family will fall apart, his children will distance themselves from him, and despite having everything, he will have nothing left.

So friends, it is very important to give quality time to the family, spend quality time with them, build relationships well, impart values to children and take care of children. So, out of the 24 hours of your life, how much time you give to the betterment of your family is very important. So, how you spend time with family is very important because if you are happy in family, if you are able to maintain harmony very well among the family members, then you can do your work very well. You can do well.

So friends, family is an important part of life. Of life. We cannot ignore this and it is very important to give quality time to him. So it is essential to have a good time with the family, spouse, and children.

So friends, come, think what we can do for our family. First of all, create a chart and the first question on it should be, on a scale of 0 to 10, where do you rate yourself in terms of giving quality time to your family? The second question should be, what work do you do for your family?

As the third question, create a chart where you write down the plans you are making this year to improve your family segment. You can write down tasks from 1 to 6, and you can also write down these targets weekly, monthly, or yearly. Most importantly, ensure you dedicate quality time daily. If your family is stable then you will be able to do your work well. So this is our fifth aspect, friends. Write the following questions related to your family in your exercise book.

- **Question 1:** How much time do you spend with your family?
- **Question 2:** How many times do you go out with your family in a year (except 2020, because that was the Corona period)?
- **Question 3:** What measures do you take for the betterment of your family?

SIXTH ASPECT: SOCIETY

In this Wheel of Life, the sixth part of life is your society. Yes friends, the money we earn is for ourselves and our family. We get all the credit for the relationships we build and good contacts we develop. But apart from ourselves and our families, we should also think about our society. We should ask ourselves what are we giving to the society? We should not avoid our responsibilities by thinking that we do not have much to give. It is becoming difficult to run the house with whatever God has given, we will think about the society only when it is too much. Friends, this mindset is not right. If you are a reader of my book, then believe me, you are definitely capable enough to help many people. You can distribute some books, copies, pens, etc., to children living in slums from time to time. If you are interested in teaching then you can start a batch of some children for free, or by charging a nominal fee.

When you start doing something even at a small level, you will begin to see yourself and many other things differently, where you can help the deprived and neglected people of society. In this mission, you can involve your friends, or old acquaintances, and do commendable work without taking help from any enlightened class of society.

However, the regret is that while we pay attention to our families, we fail to recognize any responsibility towards society. So, friends, we must remember that along with our families, we also have a responsibility towards our society, which we cannot ignore.

So, friends, this is the sixth part — without this sixth part our life is incomplete. I have seen many people who are involved in social service, who are very few in number, but a normal person would probably not be able to completely dedicate himself to the society. However, if we, as ordinary people, can dedicate some time from the 24 hours of a day or some hours from a month or a few hours from a week to social service, then it will definitely be beneficial for both ourselves and society. In these hours, you can do a lot of things, such as planting trees, feeding the hungry, educating underprivileged children, and so on.

So friends, there are many such activities which you can dedicate towards the society, contribute in them, participate actively, make important contribution etc.

Friends, I believe that if you have spent your life without doing anything for society, then perhaps your life is meaningless. So, friends, this is what I want to say---

Now, let's practice. While doing self-analysis, first, write where you stand on the scale of your contribution to society from 0 to 10. Write down where you stand. If you haven't contributed anything to society yet, your number will be 0 on the scale. Similarly, if your contribution has been the highest, then your number will be 10, meaning you have scored 10 on the scale. Then the second question is about what you want to do for society in your life, even though you are not doing anything now, and to what extent you want to do it, write it on a scale of 0-10. Then there's Planning for the year. You can write down from 1 to 5 points for the actions you want to take for the welfare of society, for the betterment of society. Then you can make a chart based on that.

When you have determined your tasks, you will write on chart paper that you will plan for these tasks on a monthly basis, weekly basis, or daily basis. In the chart, you should leave at least 10 spaces for this, from 1 to 10, so that you can write that you want to do these tasks.

So, friends, in the end, I would like to say that God has given us life not just for ourselves but also to do good for society. There are many people like Mother Teresa, Mahatma Gandhi, many others who have dedicated their lives for the welfare of the entire society. So, friends, an ordinary person may not be able to dedicate their entire life for the welfare of society, but they can surely dedicate a few hours, a few minutes. When you do good, you will feel a sense of joy from within, and when you experience joy, you will truly be very happy, and when you are happy, you will progress in life, friends.

- **Question 1:** On a scale of 0 to 10, where do you rate yourself in terms of your contribution to society?
- **Question 2:** What is your yearly plan for the betterment of society?

- **Question 3:** What is your monthly plan for the betterment of society?
- **Question 4:** Which tasks will you choose for social service?

Thank You

□□□□

SECOND QUESTION

What Do You Want from Life?

Friends... this is the second part or question of our book where we are asking ourselves, what we want from life?

It is a big question that what do we want from life, but for this we will have to travel within and talk to many people. Some people think that they want a lot of wealth from life, but friends, if you ask those who have a lot of wealth and comforts, they say, "We don't have happiness in our hearts, we don't have joy, and we don't have good health." So there are many things for which we have to find answers in our life.

So, friends, if we talk about it, the journey from sorrow to joy and celebration is a very big one. What is sorrow? Sorrow can be physical or mental. What is joy? Joy is a physical experience like sitting in a very comfortable car. You can be happy, you can experience joy, but you can also be very sad from the heart. And then, after joy, comes the next stage, which is happiness. Happiness is a state of mind. We become happy from small things. We become happy even if we get something small.

The next part is the part of bliss. Bliss arises from the soul.

You always stay happy, you feel good. You experience joy and happiness. And the biggest stage of life is celebration, which we can also call enlightenment. When we live our lives like a celebration, our life becomes admirable to others. So, if we put it briefly, what does a human want? The desire to live in happiness, joy, and celebration is something that every human wants.

So, friends, if you do a little bit of homework and practice, you can also ask yourself the question of what you want from life?

Write at least 5-6 lines because you have to find its answer.

A good phone can bring you happiness once, but it cannot provide you with the experience of happiness in life forever. Or if you live your life like a celebration because of it, that cannot happen. So there are many things that we need to do. So, write briefly what you want from life.

What do you want from life? Because until you understand what you want from life, you won't be able to live life properly.

Thank You.

□□□□

THIRD QUESTION

What is the Goal of Your Life?

Friends, as you heard from the description of my two questions in the first two parts of the book, what is life and what do we want from life. Now when you know both the aspects, you will be able to make goals in life. Friends, you have known all the parts of life, you have known 6 parts. Despite earning a lot of wealth and having all the comforts, many people are still going to sages and saints and organizations associated with spirituality, so that they can attain the thing that can give them happiness and joy in life and they can live a life of celebration.

So, friends, this is the third question from your life, what is your goal in life?

Friends, as my life experience has taught me, goals should not be confined to just one direction. As you've learned that life has six pillars, if you integrate those six pillars into your goals, you can live a prosperous life, joyful life, and a life full of celebration. So, friends, if you want to set goals, start working on the six pillars first. It's possible that you might be feeling a lot of joy in one particular pillar, so at that time, you can work even harder. You can be happy in life even by choosing one aspect of life, you can get a lot of happiness because this is the taste, happiness and joy which is precious and is available without any money.

So friends, you can set whatever goals you want for your life. The wheel of life has 6 parts. You set life goals on all of them and slowly move forward on this journey. Like you can set goals for the maintenance of your body, you can set goals for your mind, you can set goals for your soul, you can set goals for your professional life. You can set goals for the betterment of your family, you can aim to do something for the society, because life will be perfect only when you do your work in all 6 directions, friends! However, if you want to live a celebratory life, then you'll have to increase the aspect where you're experiencing the most happiness and joy.

Friends, there are many people who become scientists. They are very happy, they enjoy life, and they feel like this is their God. This is my goal. I can live a life of celebration. To recognize oneself, to support oneself, to achieve our defined goals, we need to work on all six aspects, and gradually move towards the direction where we experience the most joy and enthusiasm, so that our life can become better and better.

So friends, this was our third question. What are your goals in life? If you identify the goals of life, you will go far ahead in life.

Thank You

□□□□

FOURTH QUESTION

Who Am I?

Friends, you will have a great journey in life if you recognize who you are. If you search this question on the Internet, on YouTube, you will find different perspectives of many people. If you are related to Hindu religion, it believes that you are not a body, you are just a soul which leaves one body and enters another body.

And by the way, there have been many great men who have interpreted this question differently. There was a great philosopher and master whose name was Osho. He used to say, "You are neither the doer nor the enjoyer; you are just a spectator." If you live with a witness mentality, you will go far in life. So friends, this is my only request to you, I pray that you ask yourself this question daily: Who am I? Recognize what your existence is. This is a bit of a spiritual field question. Hence, when you work on all aspects of life and focus on the aspect of the soul, then answering this question will become much easier.

Friends, the day we understand this and recognize the definition of our subtle life and realize who we are, then life will become like a festival.

So friends, this is the fourth question of our life which you have to analyze. The question I am telling you about is, "Who am I?" Write something about yourself. If you say, "My name is this, I am this," it's just your introduction. In reality, to know what you truly are, you need to take a small spiritual journey, friends. So the day we discover the answer to this question from life that who am I, from that day life will move in a positive direction, flowing like a celebration filled with joy and happiness.

Friends, that's what I wanted to say.

Thank You.!

□□□□

SUMMARY

Friends... In summary, I would say that this exercise book which I am trying to write will be instrumental in making your journey successful. As I began this book with the four questions of my life and the promises we made to you - that you should be eligible, the second promise we made was that it's essential to listen carefully and the third promise was that it's necessary to act consciously. And the fourth is that if this book inspires you to progress in your inner journey and achieve something in life, then you will share this knowledge with your friends, relatives, and society.

You must have really understood the 4 questions of life that we have asked you, which were, "What is life?"

We learned 6 aspects of life. After that we asked second question to life, "What do we want in life?", to which I mentioned that you want happiness, joy and celebration in life.

And the third question I asked you was, "What is the goal of your life?" You also need to work on that and the most important thing, which will lead you towards satisfaction in your life, is that "Who am I?"

Believe me, if you discover "Who am I?" then you will progress significantly in life. Thank you. With this, I conclude this book, and I am thinking of the next book whose title will be 'The 5 Principles of Life'.

When that book is ready, I will share it with you all as well.

Thank You.

□□□□